AF228566

Help the Honey Bees

by Grace Hansen

Abdo Kids Jumbo is an Imprint of Abdo Kids
abdobooks.com

abdobooks.com

Published by Abdo Kids, a division of ABDO, P.O. Box 398166, Minneapolis, Minnesota 55439.
Copyright © 2019 by Abdo Consulting Group, Inc. International copyrights reserved in all countries.
No part of this book may be reproduced in any form without written permission from the publisher.
Abdo Kids Jumbo™ is a trademark and logo of Abdo Kids.

102018
012019

THIS BOOK CONTAINS
RECYCLED MATERIALS

Photo Credits: iStock, Shutterstock

Production Contributors: Teddy Borth, Jennie Forsberg, Grace Hansen

Design Contributors: Dorothy Toth, Laura Mitchell

Library of Congress Control Number: 2018946053
Publisher's Cataloging-in-Publication Data

Names: Hansen, Grace, author.

Title: Help the honey bees / by Grace Hansen.

Description: Minneapolis, Minnesota : Abdo Kids, 2019 | Series: Little activists:
    endangered species | Includes glossary, index and online resources (page 24).

Identifiers: ISBN 9781532182013 (lib. bdg.) | ISBN 9781532182990 (ebook) |
    ISBN 9781532183485 (Read-to-me ebook)

Subjects: LCSH: Honeybee--Juvenile literature. | Wildlife recovery--Juvenile
    literature. | Endangered species--Juvenile literature. | Conservation--Juvenile
    literature.

Classification: DDC 333.954--dc23

Table of Contents

Honey Bees. 4

Status. 10

Why They Matter 16

Honey Bees Overview. 22

Glossary 23

Index 24

Abdo Kids Code. 24

Honey Bees

Honey bees live throughout the world. They are often found in forests and grasslands.

Honey bees live in 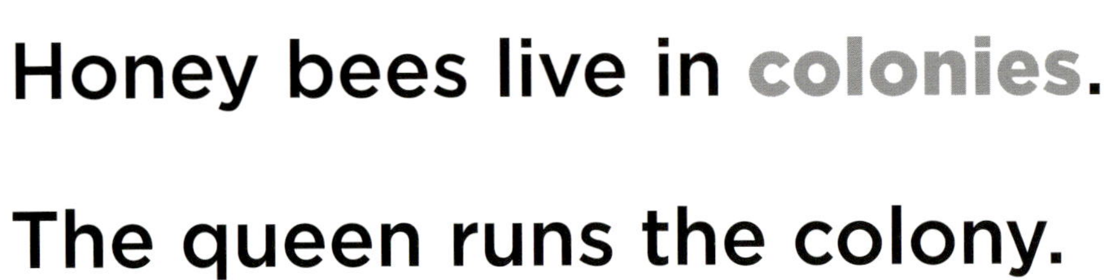colonies.

The queen runs the colony.

queen

Worker bees collect **nectar**.

They also build the **honeycomb**.

9

Status

Honey bee and other bee populations have been in decline. This is mainly because of **pesticides**.

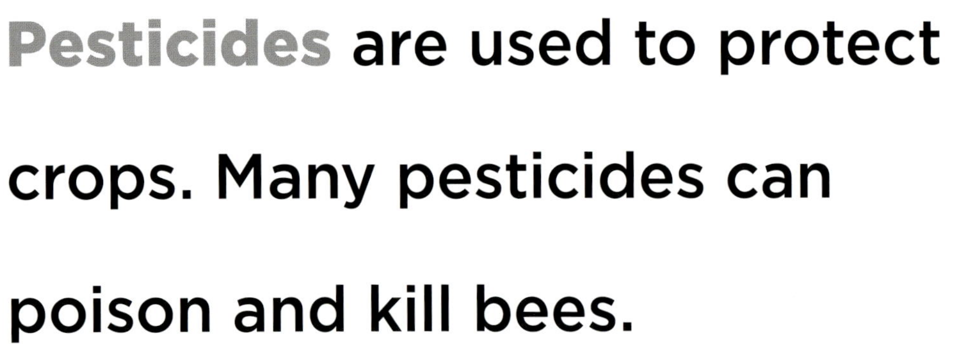

Pesticides are used to protect crops. Many pesticides can poison and kill bees.

Habitat loss is also an issue.

Bees need plants for **nectar**,

their favorite food.

14

Why They Matter

Plants need bees in order to grow. Honey bees collect **nectar** from plants. **Pollen** sticks to them when they land.

When they fly to the next

plant, they leave **pollen**

behind. This **fertilizes** the

plant. This is called pollination.

Without honey bees, many plants could not grow. Many of the crops humans rely on for food would not grow either.

Honey Bees Overview

- Status: Some populations are in decline, while others are on the rise

- Population: Around 2.89 million colonies

- Habitat: Temperate and tropical forests and grasslands

- Greatest Threats: Pesticides, habitat loss, disease, and pollution

Glossary

colony – a group of bees that live together in a large, well organized group.

fertilize – in plants, to combine male and female cells in order to make a new plant.

honeycomb – a group of many small cells made of wax in which bees store their honey. Each cell has 6 sides.

nectar – the sweet liquid a plant makes that attracts insects and birds.

pesticide – a chemical substance used to kill insects that harm plants and crops.

pollen – the fine, yellow powder made by a flowering plant. When pollen is carried by the wind or by an insect to another plant of the same kind, it fertilizes that plant's seeds.

Index

colony 6, 8

food 14, 16

forest 4

grassland 4

honeycomb 8

humans 20

plants 16, 18, 20

pollen dispersal 16, 18

queen 6

threats 10, 12, 14

worker 8

Visit **abdokids.com** and use this code to access crafts, games, videos, and more!